亚历山大·汉密尔顿

Heroes and Role Models | Non-Fiction Series

Copyright © 2022 by Level Learning, INC. and Washington Yu Ying PCS™
Original and Edited Text Copyright © 2022 by Washington Yu Ying PCS™

All rights reserved. No part of this book in whole or part may be reproduced without written permission from the publisher.

Published by Level Learning, INC.
Content Contributors:
Washington Yu Ying PCS™ - Feng Dong, Pearl Zao He You
Level Learning - Jingyao Qi

Illustrations by: Matt Austin

Leveling classification based on Level Learning standard. For full description, visit www.levellearning.com

ISBN 978-1-64040-016-0
Simplified Chinese Edition

About Level Learning:
Level Learning provides a literacy focused curriculum specifically designed for K-12 Chinese as a Second Language classrooms. Our program offers 20 levels of specific and detailed objectives, leveled texts and passages, mastery-based online assessment, and analytics to enable data-driven instruction. Level Learning reading curriculum for both literature and informational text emphasize grammar and comprehension skills to help teachers develop confident and independent Chinese language readers. The non-fiction series of books are specifically designed to support our informational text course based on multiple national standards. To learn more about our entire offering, visit www.levellearning.com.

About Washington Yu Ying PCS™:
Washington Yu Ying PCS is a Mandarin English dual language immersion International Baccalaureate (IB) World school. Yu Ying's mission is to inspire and prepare young people to create a better world by challenging them to reach their full potential in a nurturing Chinese/English educational environment. Yu Ying's comprehensive IB, dual immersion curriculum equips students with global competencies for success in the real world. As a leader in immersion education, Yu Ying is determined to advance Chinese language programs and global citizenry education by helping other schools create and strengthen their Chinese programs. For more information, email: products@washingtonyuying.org

请你看看这张十美元，你知道这上面是谁的头像吗？他的名字叫亚历山大·汉密尔顿。

1757年1月11日，亚历山大出生在一个穷人家庭。他从小就需要出去工作赚钱，穷苦的生活让他立志长大后一定要帮助穷人。

长大后,亚历山大参加了美国独立战争。他勇敢的表现得到了很多人的喜爱,华盛顿总统也很喜欢他。1789年他成为了美国第一位财政部长。

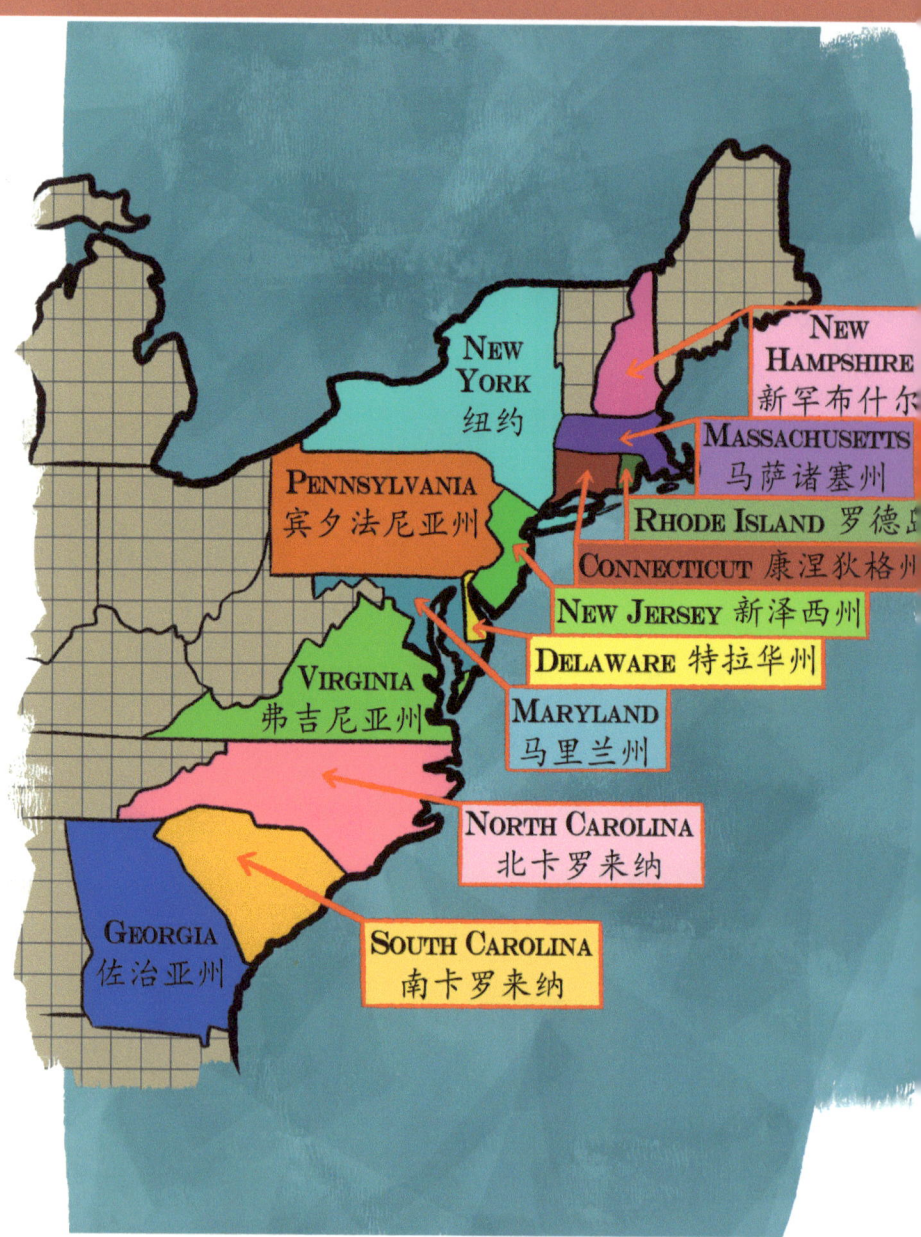

美国独立战争之后，不同的州使用不同的货币，这对人们的生活造成很大的不便。

亚历山大帮助总统成立了美国第一个国家银行。他还统一了美国的货币，大大方便了人们的生活。

亚历山大写了很多文章，建议加强美国联邦政府的重要性，这些文章对美国新宪法有很大帮助。

亚历山大真的很伟大！为了感谢和纪念他，美国人把他的头像印在了十美元上。

Glossary

	Pinyin	English Definition
头像	tóu xiàng	portrait
穷	qióng	poor
赚钱	zhuàn qián	to earn money
穷苦	qióng kǔ	poor
立志	lì zhì	determine
独立战争	dú lì zhàn zhēng	American revolutionary war
勇敢	yǒng gǎn	brave
华盛顿	huá shèng dùn	Washington
总统	zǒng tǒng	president
财政部长	cái zhèng bù zhǎng	finance minister
州	zhōu	state
使用	shǐ yòng	to use
货币	huò bì	currency
不便	bú biàn	inconvenient
成立	chéng lì	to establish

	Pinyin	English Definition
统一	tǒng yī	to unify
方便	fāng biàn	convenience
文章	wén zhāng	article
建议	jiàn yì	to suggest
联邦政府	lián bāng zhèng fǔ	federal government
宪法	xiàn fǎ	constitution
伟大	wěi dà	great
纪念	jì niàn	to remember
印	yìn	to print

www.ingramcontent.com/pod-product-compliance
Lightning Source LLC
Chambersburg PA
CBHW041225070526
44584CB00001B/101